Sorry

Lizy J Campbell

Sorry- Lizy J Campbell 2024

"Words have no power to impress the mind without the exquisite horror of their reality."
- Edgar Allan Poe

Sorry, Self

In the quiet depths of my heart,
Lies the echoes of our love's depart

Each memory, a bittersweet embrace,
Now tainted with time's relentless pace

I'm sorry for the promises I took on,
And for all the tears that I silently wept

In the shadows of what could have been,
Lies the remains of rose-colored love, once so
joyous

You failed to hold me close and dear,
And now, in your absence, my greatest fear

I have my regrets that cascade like falling rain,
Washing away hopes, never really washing the
pain

But in this failure, I find grace,

For lessons I've learned in this lonely place

I am sorry for the hurt I let you cause,

And the dreams that lay forever on pause

Though our paths may now diverge and stray,

I'll carry the weight of my burdened mistakes
every day

In the silence of this broken rhyme,

I offer my sincerest apology to myself,

ONE LAST TIME

Silver Moonlight

In the shadows cast by the moon's soft light,
a woman weeps in the still of the night

Her heart, once pure, now a tainted silver,
echoes the loss, she cannot keep on this river

Through tears that fall like whispered rain,
she morns the love she cannot regain

But her in that sorrow, a spark ignites,
a flicker of hope in these endless dark nights

With each new tear shed, her strength grows,
from ashes of pain, a phoenix rises

Her spirit, tarnished yet unbowed,
in the depths of despair, she found her own

Though her scars may mark the journey,
she rises above, her spirit unveiled
For in the crucible of grief's embrace,
she discovers her true unyielding grace

Now she walks with her head held high,
a beacon of light in the darkest sky

Tainted silver, but not undone,
a woman reborn, her battle with self, she's won

Solitude Embrace

In the depths of solitude's embrace,
I find sanctuary

Through labyrinthine corridors of the mind,
I wander, seeking solace

The gentle caress of time's touch, wounds
transform

The pain quiets,
With each new breath, a rhythm of renewal

A kaleidoscope of shattered dreams, I glean
fragments of light, stitched by moonbeams

The quiet whispers of my soul's release,
euphoria of an inner peace

In the mosaic scars, a story told, let us dance
beneath the stars

For the depths of my darkness, healing shines

Jagged Edge (Sonnet)

I'll let it be, this rift that can't be filled,
Forcing its jagged edges to stay, Unfinished,
Raw, its contours sharply milled,
If this eases your pain, I won't betray

Yet, your smile's memory I can't discard,
Your world, I was, and in my heart, you dwell,
Your tears, the battles with demons, hard,
Now, in your absence, I bid farewell

Your passing tugs at the heartstrings, vast and
tight, My hands, burdened with grief, I can't
ease the plight

In an endless stretch of time, a lifetime's worth
of sorrow, its fleeting span, Sadness
profoundly impact

An ache I cannot mime,

A void so deep, no matter the will to cover,

I am sorry to thee

Monochromatic

In laser focused wavelengths, I play

The frequency, wanted to befriend

One of pure intentions:

Honesty

We don't do drama, no bullshit here

Employ diffraction

Focused, monochromatic light

So bright

Step back, can't act,

Start the attack

Let the truths take flight

Those who are sorry, those who are on my
vibe,

glide on through

Click, in sync

Monochromatically

Values, pride

Method of payment for disrespect

Dissolves, resolves on its own

Whispers in the dark,

Emotions, like shadows in the mind,

dance,

Heartbeats sketch silence

Soft waves of sorrow,

Her essence flows out,

A river of moonlight,

Gently mending her broken shores

I'm not sorry (scream poetry)

I'm not sorry for writing a poem this way,

I need to release it; I can't let it stay

I don't care of it's popular, I don't care if these
rhyme

I don't care that you're sorry, but I do care for
all that wasted time

I'm sorry to myself for not seeing through
those lies, I am sorry I let your words
hypnotize

SORRY for anyone else feeling this way,

I am not sorry for expressing this today

That the sorry you've said:

Never paid for your crimes,

All of those memories you imposed, now I'll
have to press rewind

Stopping my grind,

Stopping my peace of mind,

Stopping my love,

Stopped in a moment, a moment in time

So, this time, this time, you don't get to repent from the scars on my mind

I'm writing this out to all who have been betrayed by fake love that temporarily made us frayed and blind

Those imprints last, longer than time

She stands tall, unyielding,

No apologies needed,

Her voice, a thunderstorm,

Reclaiming her light

Existence

In the quiet corners of her heart,

Where whispered secrets hide,

She holds a tapestry woven

With threads of sorrow and strength,

Each stitch a story of pain,

A testament to her spirit

She was taught to bend, to yield,

To say "sorry" for her existence,

To shrink herself into the shadows,

Where her light would not offend

From a young age, the world whispered, "Be less, be small, be quiet"

Her dreams, like fragile butterflies,

Were often caught in nets,

Of those who feared their flutter,

Who sought to quiet her voice,

To dim the brilliance of her being,

Afraid of what they could not control

In rooms where anger echoed,

She silences her voice,

Apologies spilling constantly from her lips

Like raindrops in a storm,

A shield from another's rage and fear

Yet within her, a fire smoldered,

Hidden beneath the ashes of apology,

A quiet, simmering strength,

A resilience set, unbroken by time

She was the moon, the tide, the earth,

Her power rooted in the core of being

Reclaimed

She stood and breathed,

a reclaiming of her space,

No longer content to whisper

Apologies for her presence

Her voice, once soft and tentative,

Now rang with the clarity of truth

She embraced her feminine energy,

A force of nature, unapologetic,

Her softness a source of power,

Her compassion, her strength

She was the wildflower in the wind,

A storm that will be tamed

Unapologetic

She no longer bowed to the shadows,

No longer whispered "sorry" to them

She rose, a beacon of unyielding light,

A warrior in her own right

And to those who once sought her out

To diminish her brilliance,

She offered neither anger nor apology,

But a quiet, resolute presence,

A reminder that true power

Needs no permission to exist

She is the dreamer and the dream,

The seeker and the guide,

In her presence, hope redeems,

And through her, her world is revived

Power, not dominance

She is the whisper of the wind,

The roar of the ocean's tide,

A force of nature, untamed, wild,

With a heart that refuses to hide

Her power is not in dominance,

She, listens to the quiet depth of her soul,

In the wisdom she carries gently,

Stories she chooses to unfold

She is the mountain's majesty,

The river's ceaseless flow,

The earth's unspoken resilience,

She is the laughter in sunlight,

The courage in the darkest of nights,

A warrior of soft strength and beauty,

Wielding her truth like light,

Unapologetic for her existence,

A voice that's loud as thunder

No more, 'sorry' in sight

Soul Song

When her soul sings, it shatters doubts

A crescendo of light and shadow,

Illuminating the path ahead

She sings of love and loss,

Of the beauty found in pain,

A testament to resilience,

Her tribute to the human spirit.

Her music is both fierce and tender,

A harmony of strength and surrender,

Echoing through the corridors of time,

Her soul song that never fades.

When the soul sings, the world listens,

Every leaf, every stone, every star,

Bearing witness to her sacred sound,

Joining and reconnecting the heart and the mind

In the quiet moments,

A lullaby of ancient echoes you can hear,

Filling the spaces between breaths,

The heart learns to dance

She dances in the light of dawn,

Feet bare upon the earth,

A celebration of her spirit,

A will in testament of her worth

A tapestry

For too long she whispered,

"I'm sorry" for being herself,

But now she dances boldly,

Embracing herself in full

Her power is in her presence,

In the courage to create boundaries,

She weaves a tapestry of change,

Created with her own two hands

She does not seek permission,

Nor bends to others' will,

She is the storm and in silence,

Like a mountain, strong and still

Rebellion

Her joy is her rebellion,

Her dance a fierce decree,

She will not be silenced,

She will always be free

In the symphony of justice,

Her rhythm is the heart,

A melody of balance,

Where every word has its part

She dances with the stars above,

And with the earth below,

A warrior, with wildflowers in her hair,

Her future grows

It feels now, so bright

She dances, cause she knows

Sorry, (Haiku)

Apologies from mouths,

Echoes of regret lingers,

Forgiveness whispers

Ode to Sorry

Oh, "Sorry," such a humble word, so often
spoken,

In moments where our hearts feel torn and
broken

You dance upon our lips with gentle voice,

A bridge between two souls,

In times of hurt, you offer solace sweet,

A balm to wounds where pain and sorrow
meet

With each utterance, burdens start to mend,

Forgiveness blooms, a flower without an end

Yet sometimes, "Sorry," wears a heavy shroud,

A mask for truths we fear to say aloud

It hides our strength, our voice, our inner fire,

Leaving unspoken what our hearts desire

But let us not diminish your true power,

For in humility, you make us flower

You teach us empathy, compassion, too,

And in your essence, we find love anew

So, here's to "Sorry," in its many hues,

A melody of healing we can't refuse

May we embrace its essence true

About the Author

Canadian Illustrator / Author Lizy J. Campbell is a self-taught artist with many interests. She is a mother of two beautiful children and has over 30 books published. She owns a publishing company called The Elite Lizzard Publishing Company in Cornwall Ontario. She illustrates children's books and paints pet portraits for people.